HOW TO BE YOUR OWN LOVER

Gain Consciousness, End Patterns, Find Happiness, and Mend Your Bonds with Others

BLAINE DAVIS

Table of Contents

Introduction - You Effect Change.

Ever attempted to halt a train in motion? I do not advise doing so. It is quite difficult to stop once it is moving and on the tracks.

Life sometimes has the same motion as that train. Everything is accelerating when you're on the tracks. fated to carry on exactly as it is.

To some extent, this mental paradigm makes sense. There is movement in your life.

You establish schedules for your job, extracurricular activities, and social interactions. You remain travelling in a specific direction thanks to these routines and habits.

There are moments in life when it seems like the train will never stop moving. difficult to halt or shift directions.

This isn't a problem when you're content and joyful. However, it's a serious problem when you feel that your life isn't progressing in the way you want it to.

Thankfully, life is not a train that can't be stopped. It is adaptive, flexible, and capable of quick change.

You could experience change.
Occasionally, something outside of yourself can throw you off balance.

As a child, this frequently occurred. You registered for new classes each semester. Every year, you advance one grade. The system was meant to change, and you responded to it.

It's not the same in the working world, though. There is no "system" in place to keep things interesting. You won't get advice from anyone on what to do next.

You may be moved to a different team. Or you could end things with your girlfriend. However, there's no predetermined pattern for how or when change will occur.

You have the power to bring about change.
Changes of the second kind are far more proactive.
You may take control of your life and make changes
instead of waiting for them to come to you.

If something in your environment isn't working, it's
up to you to try something different.

Perhaps it's beginning a brand-new exercise
regimen. or landing a new position. or embarking on
that side project you've had for a year.

You can choose to change any area of your life.

It's not always beneficial to make proactive changes
as opposed to reactive ones. Both may result in
positive or negative effects.

But the greatest approach to make sure you end up
where you want to be is to make your
transformation.

It's a game of chance as the alternative.

When things are difficult, keep going.

We've established an annual ritual of trying to bring about change. We refer to it as setting New Year's Resolutions.

But these adjustments never last. Just a tiny portion of people follow through on their New Year's resolutions!

However, this goes beyond New Year's resolutions. It has to do with each new objective or adjustment you make to your life.

It's simple to place the blame for problems elsewhere when they arise:

"The timing wasn't right,"
"By now, if this was intended to happen, it would have."
"It must not have been something I really wanted."

There are some good external explanations. However, they are typically only justifications. (And not very strong ones, either.)

The true cause of failure is surprisingly straightforward: bringing about change is difficult and uncomfortable!

Going back to your old habits is much easier when times are hard. Carrying on with your routine feels secure and at ease. We are programmed to seek security and routine.

However, staying the same isn't truly "safe." It just ensures that you will continue to carry out your routine activities.

Avoiding lucrative challenges and growth possibilities is the result of shying away from discomfort.

You can live a more satisfying life by seizing the chance to bring about your transformation.

Thus, embrace the suffering and keep going.

Make your modifications.
It's time to get to work when you feel that your life isn't leading you to where you want to be.

With this framework, you may begin bringing about constructive change. Take out a pen and notepad, and get started.

1. Decide what needs to be changed.
Find the thing you wish to give up. You may be aware of this already if you're depressed.

Start a daily journal if you're not quite sure. Avoid thinking too much about it. Spend five minutes a day writing whatever comes to mind. Once a week or two has passed, review your entries and search for any patterns of unease, melancholy, rage, or negativity.

Choose what you want to start doing in its place after you've determined what you want to change.

As an illustration, let's say you value dating and meeting new people, but your dating life has stagnated.

Making justifications for not getting together with new people is something you should give up on.
Going on dates is what you're going to start doing.

2. Permit yourself to take action.

It's simple to assign blame for your shortcomings to outside forces. However, you're likely the only one stopping yourself!

Sometimes we cling to unfavourable beliefs that hinder us:

"I'm not prepared,"
"I'm not worthy of it."
"I simply am not in the mood"
"If it were meant to be, it would have happened already."
That kind of thinking is constricting and nearly never accurate.

Permit yourself to act in lieu of them. Put it in writing. Repeat that to yourself aloud a few times.

Although it may sound corny, doing this prepares your brain for the impending change.

As an illustration, "I grant myself permission to begin dating more." because meeting new people is something I value highly.

3. Begin modestly

Making a big shift is not necessary to bring about change. When little things are done repeatedly over time, they can have a big influence.

To begin, decide on a small action you can take to move in the right direction.

This could entail sending that unresponsive person a text, downloading a dating app, or joining a Meetup group for our disgruntled dater.

All great things began as tiny beginnings.

4. Turn it into a routine

To continue pursuing your objective, concentrate on developing a habit that will last.

To keep your attention on action rather than a goal, commit to a process (e.g., going on two dates a month).

Knowing that you're moving in the right way will help you sleep well.

You are the one in control.

You could occasionally be lucky enough to receive a wonderful surprise. However, it's an erratic approach to achievement.

Thus, remember that you can bring about your change when something is bringing you down.

You are always welcome to take the wheel.

It won't be simple. However, who said that it ought to be?

This is something you can handle.

The Influence of Your Connections

That day, he attended an interview. One of the panellists questioned him, "If you graduated from so and so school, then you should know my son," after reviewing his qualifications. He studied the same material in the same year as you. "He's my friend; we were on the same research team, and we still spoke a few days ago," was his reply. The interview came to an end. He was hired!

Relationships, and friends, are crucial to your future and to moving on to the next phase of your life. In a successful economy, a relationship is an asset. Your net worth is based on your network. God places the proper individuals in your path of destiny when he wants to assist you. Additionally, the devil isolates you from important relationships in an attempt to harm you.

Perhaps the most crucial life skill to acquire is the ability to manage relationships. In the end, your relationships will define your greatness and success more than your talents or qualifications. Everywhere you look, there are gifted failures. Pastors who have been anointed are passing away in obscurity. Even now, some competent players receive pitiful compensation. The key lies in their network of contacts and relationship-serving strategies.

Except for three things—the books you read, the friends you keep, and the advice you receive—you will remain the same person throughout the next five years. Being able to relate to people well is a sign of knowledge. Your next level of greatness in life and destiny is just a phone call away. God has placed individuals in your life's path who are essential to your success. It is your responsibility to treat them.

It's essential to relationship management that you develop respect for others. Never belittle someone. You will never make a mistake if you let respect always come before yourself. Chief Naaman will teach you better; the one you despise now might be your saviour tomorrow (2 Kings 5:1-14). Remember that appearances don't always make the whole story (2 Corinthians 5:16). Sometimes, what appears to be rubbish turns out to be treasure. A prudent individual discovers the gem hidden among the debris.

I urge you to focus on building bridges rather than walls as you move on with today; walls are your roadblocks, while bridges are your means of getting to the other side of greatness. Connect with others and take care of your relationships before you need them. Make the necessary payment. Give up grudges (Luke 7:19–23, 17:1). If you wish to make friends, be amiable (Proverbs 18:24). Learn to give; you won't always desire to receive (Acts 20:35). When you need shade and fruit, the relationship tree you don't water today won't be able to supply them.

The foundation of the first Law of Combat, "Cover and Move," is the strength of interpersonal bonds. You must establish trusting bonds with people you rely on to complete your task if you are to succeed in anything you attempt.

Consider the individuals in your life with whom you truly enjoy a positive relationship. This person might be someone you work with. Or it can be a member of your neighbourhood. Anyone you truly like in your life.

What do you do when they ask you for assistance? You assist them. But what if you're preoccupied? Extremely, extremely busy? What should you do if they seek assistance? You assist them.

That is how relationships have power. It doesn't matter how busy we are as long as we have enough compassion for the other person. We'll make time to assist them.

Now think about the opposite. Consider the individuals in your life that you find objectionable. Everybody has them.

What do you do when they ask for something? Most won't take the chance. We frequently refuse to assist those we detest. Alternatively, we don't try very hard to assist them.

They are hurt by that since they are deprived of the assistance they require from you. But that also hurts you because they're on your team! For this reason, you should make an effort to establish trusting bonds with everyone in your vicinity—that is, with anyone who has the potential to have an impact on your objective.

Examining your physical appearance

Knowing who you are is the first step towards inner peace. Understanding Your Origins and Journey is the First Step Towards Becoming Who You Are.

Have you ever felt self-conscious about your appearance while you gazed in the mirror? Particularly in America, having a negative body image is frequent. Since high school, I have had difficulty maintaining a positive body image. I never thought I knew how other people saw me.

Having a mental image of oneself and others is similar to having a self-image. A person's self-image can be composed of three things: First, an individual's self-perception. The second is one's belief about how other people see them. Third, one's preferred perception of themselves. Click here to learn more about the dimensions of self-image. I constantly battle with thinking negatively about how other people perceive me. More specifically, I've always thought that other people don't find me attractive.

I've occasionally had a low physical self-image, which can lead to several potential issues, such as:

- Experiencing guilt or humiliation
- Constant self-judgement coupled with societal comparison
- Insufficient self-assurance
- Having mental health issues, such as depression

- Pursuing risky methods of altering the body, such as risky diet plans or the improper usage of hormones or supplements to gain muscle

Fortunately, there are lots of ways for people to feel better about their bodies. Their primary goal is to alter your cognitive processes or your ideas about how other people see you. These may help you alter your perception of how other people see you, but learning to accept gentler thoughts is where the true work is done. Here are some strategies you might want to try:

- Put on clothes that bring you joy.
- Refuse to listen to your inner critic.
- Don't spend too much time on social media discussing physical appearances.
-
- Make a list of the physical attributes that you find most appealing about yourself, but don't stop there!
- Be in the company of encouraging individuals.

Refrain from evaluating yourself against others.

For me, it has been easier to feel better about myself when I make small changes to my wardrobe. In high school, I seemed to have worn a lot of shorts and baggy clothing, but my mother later got me a pair of slim jeans that improved my mood. I now make a special effort to purchase thin pants from retailers since I feel more at ease and appreciate my appearance when I wear those garments. Adding more colour to my wardrobe was something else I started to do. I used to dress in dark clothes, maybe a Vikings sweatshirt, and jeans. I've come to realise that wearing more colours makes me happier. In college, I also discovered that I like working out. I only worked out in high school because it was required of me by my football team. I started to feel much better about myself once I was at ease going to the gym for enjoyment. Getting more exercise helped me start thinking better about myself.

But what worked for me might not work for you in terms of bettering your self-perception. The important thing to remember is that having bad ideas about oneself may happen to everyone. While there are strategies to help you be more optimistic, it's vital to realise that what works for me might not work for you. You may create a happy activity of your own to replace going to the gym. Consider experimenting with different looks, like a new haircut, rather than switching up your clothes. According to psychology, we can distinguish between our reality and our bad ideas. Instead of concentrating on a body portion that might not be ideal, start to see yourself as a full person.

Knowing the Neurobiology of Trauma Connections

A trauma connection is an intense emotional attachment or bond that develops between an abuse victim and their perpetrator. These kinds of ties typically flourish in situations when fear and affection coexist. The final effect is a connection that is complex and could be challenging to work through.

The first stages towards overcoming trauma bonding and achieving recovery are understanding its symptoms, causes, and recognition. This could entail calling it quits on the relationship, visiting a mental health specialist, and getting in touch with an advocate.

When Does Bonding After Trauma Occur?
Trauma bonding usually happens when the victim of abuse starts to form a relationship with the perpetrator. Not only could they form an intense emotional bond with the abuser, but they might also

come to rely on them for love, care, food, or clothing.

Similar to Stockholm syndrome, trauma bonding can occur over days, weeks, or months and is impacted by the degree of abuse, the length of the abuse, and the individual's ability to cope. Having said that, it's crucial to remember that a trauma connection never occurs because of the victim.

Although trauma bonding can happen in practically every abusive environment involving an imbalance of power, there are a few situations when trauma bonding is more likely to happen. Among the instances are:

- Abuse in the home
- Abuse of children
- Incestuous relationships
- maltreatment of the elderly
- Situations involving kidnapping or hostages
- Trafficking in persons
- Cults or extreme forms of religion
- Abuse at Work

Why Does Bonding After Trauma Occur?

The underlying urge for attachment in humans is the source of trauma ties. Trauma bonding typically happens when the victim of abuse feels intimidated and is subjected to severe treatment mixed with loving and compassionate deeds. They also tend to be closed off to other people's viewpoints and think there is no way out of their predicament.

The rational portion of the person's brain does not react under these abusive and distressing circumstances. Rather, other brain chemicals that deal with fear take over and block the part of the brain that makes rational judgments, leaving the part responsible for guaranteeing survival in charge.

Attachments begin to form because this survival brain, often known as the amygdala, is more preoccupied with survival than with reason. The outcome is a highly complicated scenario where comfort and terror coexist in a partnership.

A person's brain and cognitive processes are also altered by prolonged exposure to this type of interaction, which frequently leaves the victim feeling numb and alienated from oneself. Chasing a strong emotion is the main focus of feeling anything.

This intensity and familiarity could be what maintains the victim's attachment to the abuser.

Additionally, there is evidence to suggest that those who are extremely empathic and have experienced abuse may be more likely to bond over trauma. This may also be the reason for their inability to identify the abuse they are subjected to and their tendency to place the responsibility on themselves. However, more investigation is required to pinpoint the precise relationship between trauma bonding and empathy.

Hazards of Trauma Bonding

Additionally, some people are more prone to trauma bonding than others. For example, the following traits may increase a person's risk of developing a traumatic attachment with an abusive person:

- possess an insecure attachment
- suffered abuse as a child
- growing up in toxic relationships
- possess insufficient social support
- Show indications of low self-worth

Signs of Trauma-Based Attachment

People can be influenced by trauma in a variety of ways, even though everyone reacts to it differently. Trauma, for example, can have covert, sneaky, or negative effects. These are a few of the more prominent responses to trauma that people may experience:

Emotional responses: An individual who has gone through trauma may exhibit rage, fear, anxiety, grief, and shame. Additionally, individuals could have a numbing response in which they seem unaffected by their memories, actions, or ideas. They frequently suffer from emotional instability as well.

Physical reactions: Following a traumatic event, a person may have persistent or transient physical symptoms. For example, they can have trouble sleeping. Additionally, gastrointestinal, cardiovascular, neurological, musculoskeletal, respiratory, and dermatological diseases are frequently experienced by them.

Cognitive reactions: Persistent memories and thoughts are among the most prominent cognitive reactions to trauma. A traumatised individual may also mistakenly justify, idealise, or rationalise the actions of the abuser, especially if the abuser was a partner or carer.

Behavioural responses: Traumatised individuals are more likely to self-harm, including suicidal thoughts. Additionally, they could engage in avoidance behaviours or change how they behave in an effort to prevent abuse from occurring in the future. They could develop problems with substance misuse.

The Aftereffects of Trauma Bonding

Trauma bonding can affect an individual in a variety of ways. However, one important side effect is the overabundance of cortisol. When you are under stress, cortisol is often released to give you energy. However, frequent misuse causes your body to overproduce cortisol, which can weaken your immune system, increase your susceptibility to sickness, and raise your blood pressure.

An extensive range of additional health problems can also arise from a trauma bond. Studies have indicated that many conditions such as depression, fibromyalgia, and asthma can all be brought on by maltreatment. The following are some other effects of trauma bonding:

- protecting or making justifications for the person who injured you
- separating from friends or family
- blaming oneself or thinking that the violence is something you deserve
- being drawn to dishonest individuals
- Going above and above to support those who have wronged you
- trying to win folks over even when it's obvious they're abusing or mistreating you
- Keeping in touch with individuals you know will make you feel worse.
- Believing those who have shown themselves to be unreliable
- being unwilling to end toxic relationships
- Attempting to communicate with those that are unwilling to do so
- trying to persuade a non-listening person that anything is wrong
- Keeping in touch with someone who has mistreated you despite their refusal to accept responsibility

- being fixated on a deceased person who has caused you pain or suffering despite their absence
- Keeping your word to those who have harmed or deceived you
- concealing information concerning abuse or exploitation

How to Sever a Trauma Connection

Acknowledging the necessity of severing a trauma bond may be the most difficult aspect of the process. But you must start with creating a strategy as soon as you decide to call it quits on the relationship and move on. In order to protect themselves, abusers frequently go to considerable measures to maintain a relationship, so you should set some groundwork beforehand.

Begin by surrounding oneself with professionals. This could entail getting in touch with friends, advocates, members of support groups, or mental health specialists. The important thing is that you have a network of people who will assist you in getting ready to depart.

Think about creating a safety plan. You can get assistance from someone who has dealt with abusive circumstances and knows how to leave them securely when you are trying to figure out what steps to take to get out of the relationship safely.

Make a clean break: It's critical to walk away from abusive relationships without turning back after you've decided to do so. Attempting to resolve the situation or announcing your impending departure will just make your plan less effective. Additionally, you ought to try your hardest to break off all communication. To think clearly and help your brain become more rational, you need this time apart.

Keep yourself safe and take care of yourself: When you leave an abusive relationship, your safety and well-being should come first. Think about making both personal and practical changes—like learning to value and appreciate yourself—like changing your phone number and securing your internet safety. Knowing where to look for mental health care and where to go in an emergency can also be useful.

How to Recover From Adversity Bonding

While it is true that trauma attachments can appear difficult to break, it is possible to heal and move on with patience and time. Having a strong support system and the assistance of a licensed mental health professional are the greatest ways to do this.

Individual therapy may not only help you heal, but it can also help you learn fresh perspectives on both yourself and other people. Even when you're feeling conflicted about your relationship ending, you'll learn to embrace yourself for who you are, accept where you are in life, and be honest with yourself. Just keep in mind that this is a lengthy road. But healing is possible if you work at it.

Remember that healing is a very personal process as well. You can create a strategy with a mental health expert on how to recover from the abuse you endured. Stated that some people benefit from cognitive behavioural therapy (CBT), while others might benefit from dialectical behaviour therapy (DBT). In reality, DBT is frequently applied to those undergoing trauma recovery. The important thing is

that you're getting the support you require to recover
and feel good about yourself.

Observing Your Conditioned Self

Before you approach liberation, understand the extent of your conditioning. Ideas of independence are often veiled by training, making it simple to deceive oneself. In the absence of conditioning, freedom exists.

My glasses and conditioning go hand in hand. It modifies my perception, but I am unable to see how it is being modified. Conditioning just does what it does—unconsciously moulding, etc.—and is neither inherently "bad" nor malevolent. However, if you are unaware of its workings, your perceptions will be misinterpreted, leading to inconsistent feelings and actions. For instance, a deeply ingrained conditioned assumption that ties the mind to identity formation is the idea that security may be found in associating oneself with various concepts such as a nation, religion, style of music, football team, etc. Alternatively, more quietly, with "truths" you have discovered via experience. Still, these are concepts, not real things. To illustrate this, let's use football as an example. In reality, several men are sprinting after a blown-up leather piece in a painted area with metal poles at either end. Only a conditioned perspective might assign importance to this odd behaviour. Upon witnessing this sport, a Martian might rapidly conclude that there is no sentient life on Earth.

Avoid the misconception that conditioning is solely a cerebral, philosophical construct that ignores our feelings and instincts. These ideas give rise to the belief that our intuition or "gut" can be trusted. If sensations and emotions aren't resistant to training, then what else is?

"How is the mind set free?" is our issue. Is it possible to completely release the mind—that is, to liberate it from both the conscious and unconscious minds—rather than only releasing it in small, discrete pieces here and there or in layers? Or will the mind ever be formed or conditioned? Whether the mind can ever be free is something you have to discover for yourself; don't wait for me to tell you. Is the mind limited to thinking about freedom in the same way that a prisoner does, meaning that it is destined to remain imprisoned in the bonds of its conditioning forever?

Do you know what the issue is? Is complete freedom possible for the mind, or is mental conditioning ingrained in the mind by nature? If being restricted is the basic attribute of the mind, then there is no way to ever know what reality is. You may simply keep saying things like "there is God," "there is no God," "this is good" and "that is bad," all of which fit into the cultural mould. However, you must investigate if the mind is truly capable of freedom to learn the truth. It's up to you to decide whether or not I'm right when I claim it can be. It might be my view, my whim, or my illusion, or it might be true. Furthermore, you cannot build your life around the discovery, illusion, whim, or simple notion of another person. You need to research it.

The Trick is Done by Conditioning

Avoid embracing the concept of the unconditioned. This notion is also a result of conditioning. It is conditioned to think that conditioning is "bad," as it follows that conditioning must be "good," once we have labelled it as such. However, because it is a concept, it is not "what is," and to transcend conditioning, one must focus on "what is." What the senses can genuinely directly perceive is "what is." It is the unjudging present-moment experience of whatever is going on, be it the motion of the clouds or the sea, or an emotion like joy or rage.

Remember that you are a product of conditioning. The trick is done by conditioning. The first step is to obtain this. As with a magic trick, the real thing is not what appears to be happening. Magicians "fool" their audience by taking advantage of this weakness in everyday perception.

In what way does conditioning deceive? Although most people think of perception as being objective, logical, and passively absorbing the world around them, training actively contributes to misconceptions and deceptions. Thus, we typically think that we are seeing an objective reality in our day-to-day experiences. However, what if the process of conditioning creates both the perceiver and the perception? This can confuse perception, making it appear as though "objective reality" is supporting my beliefs and worldview while, in reality, what is happening is self-validating conditioning.

Is there a reason so many individuals reject the disruption of changing to what is new and different in their lives and instead form a fixed vision of what is true, real, essential, etc. in their world? "What the human being is best at doing is interpreting all new information so that their prior conclusions remain intact," Warren Buffett once said.

When reality knocks on someone's door and challenges a deeply held belief or assumption, it can be shocking. When a relationship is characterised by a stubborn refusal to acknowledge reality, the same thing could be stated. Although the knowledge you have amassed may have some value, it pales in comparison to the infinitely unpredictable flow of life. When you recognize your "certainties" for what they are, a sound mind may conclude that the vast majority of the unknown provides protection.

Making Use Of Your Body's Wisdom

I used to be proud of being among the most rational individuals I know.

Throughout school, I was both complemented and made fun of for being "that brainy kid," so I took that to indicate that my mind was the most important and trustworthy tool I had.

I considered it foolish to believe anything in the absence of unquestionable proof. I never gave non-logical or practical options any thought at all. And when my intuition told me something different from what I wanted to believe, I suppressed those feelings.

Years later, I hardly recognize that old version of myself, but I can see now why she gave her logical thinking such a high priority.

Our contemporary civilization has developed an obsession with the intellect, reason, and the human mind.

A three-step procedure, a comprehensive pros/cons list, statistical information, a coherent justification, and a step-by-step action plan with consistent results are what we seek.

And while there's nothing at all wrong with desiring those things, the issue lies in the fact that we now prioritise logic over all other methods of obtaining data and making decisions.

Though there are other excellent tools for navigating the world besides logic... additionally, it's not even the strongest one.

Your body is the greatest untapped reservoir of wisdom you possess, provided you allow it to be there constantly.

Your body is wise, but your mind is incredibly intelligent.

Your intellect cannot begin to imagine the depth of wisdom contained in your physical body.

It continuously detects minute clues from the environment around you, things your conscious mind is completely unaware of, and tries to convey them to you through bodily experiences and emotions.

Because of this, even before you are aware of your fear, you can feel the hairs on the back of your neck spring up.

This explains statements like "It just felt like a bad gut feeling," "That place has great energy," or "My whole body lit up when I saw that person."

Sadly, a lot of us have a tendency to dismiss or disregard these messages since our logical minds can't make any sense of them. However, such does not lessen their validity.

Equally significant to the mind's knowledge is the body's wisdom, which is always attempting to direct you toward higher states of comfort, contentment, wellness, passion, and joy.

Finding a Balance Between Your Mind's Intelligence and Your Body's Wisdom

Imagine your body as a highly sensitive, precisely calibrated compass guiding you towards health, joy, and peace, and your mind as an incredible, complicated, highly advanced computing machine.

You should think about stuff like this.

Resolving a workplace logistics issue, organising projects, organising a vacation or event, or picking up a new skill or technique.
However, you should listen to your body's advice in deeper, more emotional, and purpose-driven situations. Items such as...

Investigating your hobbies and passions,
In search of greater contentment in your life and profession,
Making an effort to strengthen your bonds with others or make new connections,
In search of inspiration for creative work,
or trying to decide what you should accept and what you should reject.

When you attempt to use reasoning to navigate circumstances that call for the deeper knowledge of your body and intuition, you'll wind up overanalyzing the problem, feeling trapped, and not coming to the optimal conclusion. just as a result of utilising the incorrect instrument.

Your Body Won't Be Disregarded
It's your responsibility to ensure that the constant communication your body has with you is two-way.

Your body is sending you signals, but if you keep ignoring them, they won't go away. They will only become more insistent and louder until you are unable to ignore them any longer.

For instance, a friend of mine had a stressful year due to a toxic workplace, several family health difficulties, and little time for herself. During almost the whole year, she developed hives all over her body.

But within days of starting to prioritise alone recharge time after accepting a new job, the colonies vanished.

In addition, the longer my clients stayed in an unsatisfactory relationship, job, housing arrangement, or any other circumstance, the more their bodies revolted against them.

Some of them would get migraines regularly, while others would experience panic attacks, gastrointestinal problems, or even long-term illnesses. all of which would vanish when they quit their jobs, moved, changed their living arrangements, etc.

However, you may pay attention to your body's signals and obey them without waiting for it to go into full-blown rebel mode. It won't have to use such painful tactics to attract your attention if you're paying attention to the early, subtle signals it keeps sending you.

How To Begin Hearing Your Body Speak

In order to regularly access that deeper intuitive understanding, here are some easy techniques to begin attuning to your body (during the earlier, subtle stages):

Start observing how your body responds to various people, things, places, and circumstances throughout the day. Do you feel queasy when you have to speak with a specific coworker? When you enter the neighbourhood coffee shop, does your body feel completely at ease? When you learn about a fresh opportunity, does your pulse beat faster and faster? When someone extends an invitation to a function, do you experience anxiety or tension? You shouldn't disregard these important signals from your body because they are all present!

Inquire about your body about its current requirements and desires. Find out what your body wants to eat before you head out for lunch. Ask your body what it wants to wear that day before you put on any clothes. Ask your body what kind of workout it needs right now before you start exercising. Your body will give you a distinct response, which is probably going to vary slightly each day.

Check-in with your body before taking advice, criticism, or opinions from other people at any time. Your body always understands what's true for you, even when your mind often becomes overwhelmed and confused by the abundance of information available to it. See how your body reacts to suggestions before assuming it would be beneficial for you. Does their advice sound repulsive and disgusting? Or do you find their proposal intriguing and stimulating? In most cases, your intuition is correct.

Bringing About Change Thru Consciousness

Our current, ever-changing state of mind shapes the reality we inhabit.

Similar to an energy field, a state of consciousness draws in circumstances and feelings that strengthen it in turn.

For instance, you'll probably start to notice or create new issues in your life if you're upset about not exercising enough or a bad remark you overheard. If you spend all day on Facebook without adding value to your life or the lives of others, you will feel empty and this will have an impact on everything else you take to be true.

Losing one's heart and concentration
When we allow ourselves to get sidetracked and lose sight of our goals, our body loses energy, our old habits resurface, and our drive wanes. Furthermore, when we are low on energy, we are more likely to attract ideas and emotions that lead us to feel as

though we are not even interested in pursuing our true desires. This is misleading!

"Oh, I'm not in the right frame of mind."
"Maybe I'm not this kind of person after all."
"Later, I will do that."

This might lead to a great deal of confusion at times. "I truly wanted to go forward and I was prepared to do this, so why do I feel as though I no longer want it?" As though I abruptly changed completely and had a different destiny.

Many of us just keep going through the same cycle over and over again, but some people might be lost in that hole for years if they identify with their sensations and begin to support this fleeting reality with their thinking.

We open our eyes and everything seems perfect for a while. We are aware of our identity and goals. Our deepest desires are tied to ourselves, and we make strong progress in that direction. We are certain of our course. We are incredibly inspired, passionate, and creative; everything is going so well. There doesn't seem to be much work involved in any of the steps because we are so energetic.

However, all of a sudden, we lose awareness and enter a realm of transient pleasures and diversions that do not nourish our souls. If the energy has vanished, this is when emptiness and darkness begin to appear. We feel disoriented, go through an identity crisis, and lack motivation. Not enough strength to do anything. Instead, we prefer to be heedlessly indolent and divert our attention with thoughts of binge eating, having sex, purchasing, consuming, and viewing fascinating television.

We succumb to egoistic and frequently self-destructive practices that, while they may appear quite valuable at the time, we know deep down that they are only a gradual death with no true worth. When in such a level of consciousness, a person could forget that pleasure is an internal endeavour and instead begin looking for love outside of themselves.

The ramifications of this derailment depend on when we become aware of our lack of attention and how long we allow it to persist. Long-standing habits may have a significant impact on this. Some people are more able than others to return to deliberate and reasonable behaviour, but if someone is not well-versed in self-management and is accustomed to staying in their comfort zone, they may become trapped for days or even weeks until something compels them to move.

"People are as lazy as they are allowed to be" is a very true phrase if one is disconnected from one's own purpose and essence.

What facilitates people's escape from the hole?
Fear and responsibilities cause our survival instincts to take over and tell us to complete our assignments or report to work. While it is helpful in that it gets us moving, it is only a part of the answer. We are not satisfied when we follow norms out of fear and lack of own vision.

Emotions such as frustration, despair, and rage can be powerful agents of change, but how and where they are directed will determine the outcome. It can occasionally be so strong that it instantly tosses us across the river. These strong emotions have great power because they force us to make decisions that could result in happiness or pain, freedom or incarceration, or life or death. Someone decides categorically, "I MUST change!"

Constant emptiness, self-suppression, and self-deception don't solve anything, but strong, difficult feelings are what will always enable us to get out of the mess we find ourselves in. Thus, rather than being afraid of or suppressing our emotions, we should be thankful for them! The soul speaks through emotions.

But must we wait until outside forces compel us to take action? Must our souls rend in agony before we make a shift in behaviour?

Of course not, which is why experiencing life is so wonderful. Every moment, we can alter our consciousness. With a simple finger flick, we can return to the new world and wake up.

Our entire reality is our responsibility. But we have to acknowledge this first. To truly appreciate the enormous power we have within us, we must go through it ourselves.

Consciousness

When you meditate or practice mindfulness, you observe your thoughts, feelings, and experiences with the same objectivity and detachment as if you were watching a play on a big screen.

Being conscious is the ideal place to start, as it enables us to look at the circumstances more critically and to stop digging ourselves deeper holes of sorrow. We simply notice the experience and acknowledge that we have the power to change it whenever we choose, without passing judgement on ourselves or believing that the current reality will stay forever.

However, awareness is only a necessary first step. We require courage to take a risk and venture outside of our comfort zone while we're entangled in a thick web of spider webs. It will need some start-up energy to avoid sabotaging ourselves (by shutting off the web browser, getting up, or going outside).

It is insufficient to have fleeting ideas or recollections of our goals, principles, and prior experiences when we have descended into a poor mental state and lost touch with our passions. "I am conscious of these mental delusions. I am aware that this is only a transient situation. I know what's right and what I truly want, so why am I still standing where I am?

Vibrations and energies make up all life. A concept doesn't feel true if it doesn't align with our current consciousness. We must thus increase our energy levels before anything else.

Achieving the appropriate level of awareness
How can one alter one's awareness to generate novel ideas, feelings, convictions, and experiences?

Movement is the intake of oxygen, blood, fresh air, and a wider perspective. With your body, what are you doing? How are you doing? How do you move, and where are you now? It has a big impact on our energy levels. For instance, when we allow our backs to drop into the chair, it's not because we're lazy; rather, our body's posture contributes to our laziness.

Every step has a meaning and an intention: our actions convey the narrative of the kind of people we aspire to be.

Silence, spaciousness, and presence during meditation. the ability to release old habits and limitations and establish a connection with your own self.

Your mind will be more at ease when you breathe more deeply and slowly. You can alter your perception by altering your breathing.

Gratitude Reflection: Connecting with another person's enthusiasm (a well-written piece, film, video, or book). something that evokes emotions. A constructive energy exchange helps you to remember your goals and principles.

How fresh, how hydrated, and how easily digestible is the food? Food has the potential to either put us to sleep or give us strength and vigour.

Sleep: A calmer, brighter mind results from deep sleep. Sleeping too much sleep makes you feel like a zombie, but staying in tune with nature's rhythm—going to bed early and rising up with the sun—makes you feel creative.

Physical Space: How tidy and well-organised is your room? Living a more minimalistic lifestyle makes it easier to concentrate on the important things in life because anything in your field of vision wastes valuable mental energy.

Inspirational music, like the songs on my PowerMusic playlist, helps us remember who we are and what we are capable of.

Additional Techniques: thankfulness, singing, positive affirmations, visualisations, and all other enjoyable pursuits.

It all boils down to FOCUS: our world is ultimately shaped by our thoughts and where we focus.

We have countless chances to alter our minds and build a brand-new universe. But occasionally, just performing these easy actions might demand a great deal of willpower. a wise selection and judgement. Everything relies on where you begin and how much momentum you already have. It is always simpler to turn around when you make your first mistakes or lose awareness.

This is our opportunity to develop our self-control and willpower. Why wait for better circumstances when we are such powerful beings? Everything is now able to be changed!

If you are weak in willpower, it makes sense to begin with the smallest, most straightforward activity. What is the least demanding energy that can result in a fresh start?

That is, to me, breathing. Taking my first steps. putting the computer and other distractions away. Either clicking the X with the mouse or pressing the Shutdown button. It's not as hard as it sounds.

Your soul will eventually begin to awaken, and momentum will begin to build. All that's left to do is keep your eyes open and let the snowball fall.

Every person is a genius just waiting for the ideal environment to be unleashed. Give him/her a chance, and wonders will begin to occur!

Unlocking Your Heart's Potential

One can only discover the truth of love by searching within oneself. Since the heart is the organ through which we connect to everything, it is thought to contain the eternal secrets of love. Love passes through the sacred location located in our hearts to enter and exit our physical bodies. It is present in every organ, cell, and atom in the body, but it does not call any of these places home. The heart is only a translator of love; it cannot hold the immensity of love.

Everything we require to love and be loved is within us from birth. We are hardwired to communicate with the universe, thus our sacred coordinate comes with a USB connection. Our upbringing, education, friendships, parental values, and the love and care we get as infants all have an impact on how receptive our hearts become. Since love is the highest kind of wisdom in the universe, a closed heart is worse than a closed head.

Love Can Only Enter or Leave With An Open Heart.

The portal to love is the heart. Love can only enter or escape an open heart. The quantity of love that can flow depends on how much this heavenly portal is opened. A completely open heart permits an unrestricted and boundless flow of love. It makes room for love to fill every part of our lives and selves. Although an open heart is brimming with love, it is not a container for love. The heart cannot hold love, yet the boundless flow of love keeps the heart full all the time. Love is a never-ending stream that never stops. It is uncontainable. Love is everywhere, yet it never truly stays somewhere.

Love is not able to flow freely from a closed heart. It isolates a person from other people and the outside world. Its possessor is isolated, confined, and repressed by it. The brightness in the heart fades. The restricted amount of information that light can convey prevents consciousness from rising, which causes the heart to close even more. It is rare to consider loving oneself. A vicious circle is established.

The Secret To Opening Your Heart's Door Is Loving Yourself

Self-love lies at the core of the human heart. You are the most important person to love and be loved by. Without self-love, self-realisation is an internal task that can never be successful. We ignore the most significant voice of all when we listen to other people's opinions about who we are—whether they come from the government, the media, the internet, friends, family, church, or any other place.

To be self-loved is to value and respect oneself sufficiently to prioritise one's feelings and thoughts. It also calls for us to celebrate our divine perfection and wholeheartedly accept our imperfections as human beings.

With our unique set of gifts just ready to be shared with the world, every one of us is an important member of the creation. Every "gift from God" originates in the heart. Love is the giver and a gift that only the heart can embrace. Each time we listen to our hearts, we are using our talent. We live our truth and manifest our divine uniqueness in the world when we follow our hearts.

A true act of self-love could resemble this:

"So here I am, world, in all my beauty, following my calling, no matter what others may say. I came for two reasons: to share my special gift with the world and to live a happy life as I believe that's how I'm supposed to live. I came to do what I love.

When we embrace, adore, and appreciate who we are, our hearts open out wide.

Our Contagious Love for Life and Everything in It

An open-hearted person exudes a glow because of the strength of their heart's electromagnetic field. Our consciousness can grow as more light enters our hearts and more information flows in. We have an infectious love for life and everything in it. We become magnetic and draw the things we require to follow our hearts. A pattern of growing happiness, plenty, thankfulness, and love is established. We turn into "shining examples" of completely sincere individuals.

Naturally, our hearts are open when we are joyful. We reconnect with love and remember who we are. Because our heart light is shining through, we "beam with joy." We shine. We glow intensely, which is a real indication of an open heart.

Living as the god that we are means creating through love, if God creates through love. We also need to have an open heart for it. To make sure that only those with open hearts have the greatest creative ability, the universe has put in place several checks and balances. The secret to successfully navigating these checks and balances is self-love.

We Must Love Ourselves to Receive Our Divinity

How to Open the Door to Your HeartWe are unable to tap into the full potential of our heart's electromagnetic field unless we learn to appreciate who we are. Our hearts are open to receiving more light when we adore who we are. Our heart's electromagnetic field becomes stronger as more light enters it, increasing the possibility that our dreams may come true. The basis for generating our wants is self-love.

To access our divinity, we must learn to love ourselves. This entails loving both our heavenly and human selves. To become the actual co-creators that we are, we must learn to appreciate every aspect of who we are.

You have to learn to love the wonderful energy that is you. To love the god within you with all of your heart, mind, and spirit is to love yourself as the god that you are.

"Being open to oneness means being honest with yourself in your heart." It's about getting sucked into your love. It is the most personal manifestation of the experience of love.

You fall in love with all of creation when you fall in love with the god that you are.

A Real Chance at Self-Empowerment Is Now
It is an entirely new paradigm to live as the deity that you are. You are in tune with the deity when you live as the deity that you truly are. God, the One Source of All, is a part of you. You are the heart, hands, and eyes of God. The coordinated motion of

the creation's particles has ensnared you. The universe is waiting for your order.

live in the purity of this moment, live as the deity that I AM. Since matter is created in the present, the only thing that "matters" is the present. You acknowledge and accept the perfection of every moment. Every moment, you can bring about the things that your heart truly desires, making sure that everyone's best interests are met.

It's time to accept responsibility for our world if it is true that we make it. I can respond. I have power. God is me in human form. I adore the person I am! Time for genuine self-empowerment, please.

Discovering The Greatest Wisdom Deep Within Your Heart: You Are Divine

The reality of who we are is filled into our hearts when we elevate our vibration and consciousness. When we accept who we are, we come to understand that everything is inside of us, which is why the heart is considered to be full. All of these things are within: God, the zero-point energy field, cosmic consciousness. The field that passes through us is a part of ourselves. The mystics have told us that we are all connected for this reason. We are all connected to this web of energy by countless whirling vortexes.

"What might make you void, that is an illusion that you have created? You are in the Universe, and the Universe rests within you. What more could you ask for?

We all own the secret to realising our deepest desires. We need to use this key to unlock the door first. It is not the key that needs to be unlocked, but rather our heart field. Living like the gods that we are is the key.

Discovering the deepest wisdom you possess—that you are divine—in your heart is the key to unlocking the mysteries of creation. In human form, you are God. You realise that you are always connected to Source, thus concepts like hope and trust become meaningless. Your heart is always full of possibilities, joy, amazement, thankfulness, and love when you live as the god that you are and know yourself to be.

Getting The Affection You Desire

Everyone is entitled to wholesome partnerships. Healthy relationships, however, are developed over time, with each member actively sculpting a dynamic that is either healthy or ill. They don't just happen. What is the main factor influencing the relationship's quality? the actions of every individual.

Regretfully, not many of us receive the same open instruction on healthy interpersonal behaviours as we do on how to operate a motor vehicle or engage in safe sexual activity. Because of this ignorance, we are more likely to find ourselves in harmful relationships—something that may occur without our conscious awareness.

The good news is that healthy habits can be developed and put into practice with friends, partners, or family members at any age and in any kind of relationship. And you can observe changes without doing a total overhaul of your life. A healthy dynamic can be created in a relationship by making even the tiniest self-empowerment move. Here are four easy ways you can start putting healthy relationship practices into practice right now.

1. Express "No" Without remorse

It's difficult to say "no" to someone you care about, especially if you're the type of person who prefers to avoid controversy and maintain harmony by being overly accommodating. People-pleasers frequently go to uncomfortable measures to maintain their good-girl or good-boy image and avoid unpleasant labels like "rude" or "selfish," driven by a need to win acceptance and avoid conflict.

Regrettably, if you always prioritise meeting the demands of others over your own, it will negatively impact both your relationships and your well-being. You become a doormat that people may trample all over. In relationships, negative emotions like resentment, helplessness, rage, and frustration simmer beneath the surface until they explode. People-pleasing can eventually make you more vulnerable to more destructive manipulation techniques if someone with bad intentions realises they can use it to manipulate you into doing what they want. In these situations, "small" requests will probably become demands with bigger consequences as your relationship develops.

Both partners should feel as though their needs are acknowledged, respected, and taken care of in a healthy relationship. You should never feel forced to say "yes" when you truly want to say "no," especially when doing so goes against your needs or ideals. It should never be one-sided when one party always caves in.

It's acceptable to say "no," people-pleasers everywhere take note. That's not only acceptable—it's healthy to say "no." It doesn't make you a bad person to say "no." It indicates that you value yourself highly enough to respect your priorities, boundaries, and requirements. This kind of self-respect not only sets the stage for healthy relationship dynamics but also sends a strong signal to others that you are deserving of respect.

How can you begin to refuse? Give yourself enough time to process a request first. You won't feel under pressure to say "yes" right away if you put off deciding for an hour or a week by saying, "I'll get back to you," or "Let me check." Additionally, it allows you the opportunity to connect with your own needs and that sometimes elusive "gut" feeling, ensuring that you give your own best interests due consideration.

When the time comes to say "no," practice a few go-to responses in case you become tense or lose your words. Some examples are "Unfortunately, that doesn't work for me," "I've given it a lot of thought, and I'm not going to be able to," or just "No, I'm unavailable."

You are under no need to explain your decline, even though you have the option. Try to avoid the need to over-explain or add "I'm sorry" to the start or finish of your statement; a simple "no" will be enough. For many of us, it's a force of habit, but honestly, is there any reason to feel guilty about attending to your personal needs? A hint: Don't do that!

2. Decide What You Want and Own It

Overly agreeable decision-making, particularly when it comes to letting others decide for you, can also create an environment that is conducive to the growth of toxic relationships. Delegating modest choices like what movie to watch could also seem insignificant, much as accepting small favours might seem harmless. "It doesn't really matter to me, so I'll just let someone else decide," is one possible thought.

The problem arises when you begin to assign decisions regularly, establishing priorities and creating opportunities for exploitation and manipulation. Let's take an example where you always let your friend choose the movie for your weekly movie night. She eventually stops requesting your opinion and decides for herself. One day, however, her boyfriend shows up at your movie night. She tells me that she didn't think it would be a big deal because you're such a mellow person and don't even mind what movie you watch. You are so laid back that you overlook him interrupting your time with your best friend, despite your irritation. Are you not?

Here, your friend thought that you would react the same way if she were to choose the movie on your movie night based on your behaviour in one situation—choosing a movie—and extrapolate it to another. Giving someone else constant control over decisions can lead to harmful expectations and pressure to act in the same way even in situations where the circumstances are different, as seen even in this somewhat harmless case.

One person shouldn't make all the decisions in a healthy relationship; if it has in the past, you always have the power and the right to alter it. It's possible to have some healthy challenges, especially if you're transitioning from a relatively passive role to a more assertive one. If you pick the movie this week, for instance, your friend might say something like, "Aww, I already psyched myself up about that other movie," which would be a reasonable expression of disappointment. The fact that we won't be seeing it disappoints.

But be wary of resistance that takes the form of punishment, guilt-tripping, or blaming as these are indicators of unhealthy relationships. For instance, "I don't even want to go anymore," or "I put so much time into planning this night and now you completely ruined it." Instead, I'm just going to hang out with my other buddy. It is never appropriate to make you feel guilty for constructively voicing your opinions.

Even while it would be simpler to delegate less important decisions to others, because the stakes are so minimal, these choices present excellent chances to practise assertiveness. You can voice your opinions to a friend, lover, or family member who will listen to you and respect them.

Thus, the next time a minor decision needs to be made, don't ignore it; instead, take action. You'll start to feel more empowered even if it doesn't work out perfectly—for instance, the movie you pick is a disaster—and you can use that newfound authority to make bigger, more consequential decisions in the future.

3. Speak Up When Something Upsets You
Don't let the "small" things in relationships get by without your attention. Acting in silence can be just as dangerous as putting off making little decisions for other people. It's a slippery slope that can go

unnoticed into dangerous territory when silence turns into a habit that someone else can exploit.

People often keep quiet about little things that bother them because, well, they're little and they don't think they have the right to be unhappy about something that seems little.

If you find yourself trying to rationalise away your feelings of anger, irritation, hurt, or jealousy when someone with whom you are in a relationship does something that makes you feel bad, say something like, "I know I shouldn't be angry/hurt/hurt/jealous [fill in the emotion]." RIGHT THERE, STOP.

You are entitled to experience any emotions that arise because neither you nor anybody else can control them. When it comes to handling a particular issue, there is no one-size-fits-all emotional response. Any negative feeling you have is normal and a sign that you need something you're not getting.

When these unpleasant feelings surface in a relationship, it's a good time to talk to the other person about your needs and boundaries. Try bringing up the topic without placing blame to avoid making the other person feel attacked or defensive. "I felt [insert negative emotion] when you [insert their action that caused emotion]," for instance, might be said. Addressing the little things regularly can help you build a relationship where openness and communication are valued, as well as provide you with the self-assurance and structure you need to deal with larger problems down the road.

4. Find Humour in Your Flaws

Everyone has imperfections they wish they could instantly vanish, insecurities, and blunders they commit. It comes with being a human. Furthermore, anyone who wishes to control us—whether it be a friend, spouse, or relative—will be able to identify our biggest vulnerabilities and phobias and attempt to take advantage of them.

Even if your first instinct might be to cover up your flaws from the public, the best thing you can do is accept them with pride (there's nothing quite like taking ownership of your shortcomings, right?). Making light of your shortcomings in public reduces their impact and deprives those who would try to exploit them to harm, control, or manipulate you of a potent weapon.

Laughing at your flaws also shows other people that you embrace who you are and that you hope others will too. It's like declaring, "Take it or leave it—here I am!" It's scary to be vulnerable, but a good friend, family member, or lover will love and accept you for who you are, imperfections and all.

Healthy relationships, like any other, need to be actively worked towards to become and remain that way. The best thing about these four behaviours is that you can start implementing them right away in your current relationships. But don't let their simplicity deceive you—behaviour modification is extremely tough, and you'll probably find that even the slightest step is difficult. Recognize that long-lasting change takes time, so take time to appreciate your little victories along the road and treat yourself with kindness as you learn. You'll gain more confidence and become more capable of fostering positive interpersonal relationships with practice.

Strengthening The Bonds In Your Relationships

Human connection is based on relationships, which offer love, support, and common experiences. Building the link between you is crucial for enduring relationships, whether you're looking to establish familial ties, love relationships, or friendship. Learn eight practical techniques to strengthen your bonds and create enduring partnerships.

Good communication is the cornerstone of any successful and happy partnership. It is the essential thread that unites two people and promotes closeness, trust, and understanding. We'll look at the fundamentals of effective communication in this post and offer helpful advice on how to make your connections stronger.

Active Listening: The Basis of Knowledge
It takes more than just hearing words to properly understand the needs, intentions, and emotions that are hidden beneath them. You can show your partner

that you value their opinions and feelings by carefully listening to them. This small gesture of empathy can go a long way towards creating a solid basis of trust.

Demonstrating Compassion and Validation

Healthy communication is built on acknowledging your partner's feelings, even if they are different from your own. It's an effective method of communicating the message, "I see you, I understand you, and your emotions matter." This affirmation can improve communication, establish emotional security, and fortify your bond.

Picking the Appropriate Time and Location

Effective communication requires timing. Sometimes, when feelings are running hot, it's better to wait until things are more subdued. Establish a conversation-friendly, safe, and comfortable environment for the two of you. This guarantees that talks are fruitful and beneficial.

Making Use of I Statements

A key component of good communication is avoiding accusation and blame. Try expressing your feelings using "I feel..." as opposed to "You make me feel..." This encourages understanding rather than defensiveness by turning the conversation towards your feelings.

Honouring Individuality and Distinctions

Keep in mind that you are two distinct people, each with your own viewpoints, histories, and moral standards. Accept and honour these distinctions. They give your relationship more nuance and complexity. Finding points of agreement and recognizing each other's abilities is crucial.

Two Flawed Individuals Refusing to Give Up

Imperfections are a given in any connection. Accepting them is a sign of your love and dedication. "Two Imperfect People Refusing to Give Up" represents the power that results from working together to overcome obstacles.

Constructive Conflict Management

Arguments are an inevitable component of any partnership. It's important to approach them with a positive outlook. Steer clear of criticism and blame and concentrate instead on coming up with answers and agreements that respect both viewpoints.

Fostering Transparency and Truthfulness
Communication that is open and honest fosters trust. Talk openly about your needs, wants, and feelings. This openness to vulnerability promotes intimacy and makes room for a more profound bond to develop.

Honour accomplishments and landmarks
Mutual respect is strengthened when people acknowledge and celebrate each other's accomplishments, no matter how modest. Saying "I see your efforts and I'm proud of you" is what it means.

Never Give Up Growing With Each Other
Good communication is a continuous process. Maintain open communication and a willingness to change and develop as a team. A flourishing partnership is fueled by this readiness to change.

"Communication is Key: Strengthening Your Relationship Bonds" is ultimately about valuing and fostering the special bond you have with each other. Using attentive listening, compassion, and a dedication to development, you establish a connection that is resilient to all obstacles. It's the tale of "Two Imperfect People Refusing to Give Up" and establishing enduring love.

Conclusion

As if your life relied on it, learn to love yourself! You will never have to do anything for yourself in your life that is as rewarding and challenging as it is.

True love is typically thought of being an emotion that is centred around other people. However, loving oneself is as vital to having a happy and fulfilled life. The secret, though, is to learn how to love yourself before your loved ones, friends, and other people.

Self-love is a state of being that is constant rather than an emotion, and it is an indication of emotional maturity and personal growth. Loving yourself demonstrates that you value who you are and that you realise that happiness is the most important thing. It is also an honest assessment of your value and potential, as well as taking responsibility for your progress process.

It's the capacity to love and accept oneself for who you are, appearance or behaviour included. It's the capacity to unabashedly accept who you are. You can establish limits with it.

Learning to love oneself should be a part of your self-worth, self-esteem, and capacity for happiness, regardless of your size, colour, ethnicity, or place of residence—young or old, Asian or White, Black or Hispanic, or from a large metropolis or a tiny hamlet.

It takes self-love, self-care, and mental wellness to attract and maintain a loving, healthy relationship. It is simpler to let others love us and experience the delight of receiving love in return when we love ourselves. It's challenging for us to understand and value another person's favourable feelings for us when we are insecure, don't like who we are, and focus on other unpleasant emotions instead.

Being kind, patient, and respectful towards others comes more easily when we work on our own personal growth and self-love journey. It is simpler to see the world for what it is—a lovely place full of people deserving of our love and kindness—when we are content with who we are, imperfections and all.

We can take care of our own needs and stop depending on other people to make us happy or fulfilled when we put ourselves first. We don't need help from others to take care of our emotional needs; we can take care of ourselves. And that improves us as family members by enabling us to actively support the family and have an open mind to exciting new experiences.